Mel Bay's
BLUES CLASSICS SONGBOOK

by JERRY SILVERMAN

© 2008, 1993 BY MEL BAY PUBLICATIONS, INC., PACIFIC, MO 63069.
ALL RIGHTS RESERVED. INTERNATIONAL COPYRIGHT SECURED. B.M.I. MADE AND PRINTED IN U.S.A.
No part of this publication may be reproduced in whole or in part, or stored in a retrieval system, or transmitted in any form or by any means, electronic, mechanical, photocopy, recording, or otherwise, without written permission of the publisher.

Visit us on the Web at www.melbay.com — E-mail us at email@melbay.com

Contents

Ain't No More Cane on the Brazis 62
Alabama Bound 46
Alberta, Let Your Hair Hang Low 102
All Night Long 66
Backwater Blues..................... 44
Beale Street Blues 6
Been In the Pen So Long 82
Boll Weevil Blues 108
Brown's Ferry Blues 58
Careless Love 115
Dallas Blues 9
Darlin' 86
Deep River Blues 60
East Colorado Blues 105
Easy Rider 100
Empty Bed Blues 52
Fare Thee Well 114
Frankie and Johnny 42
Freight Train Blues................... 68
Goin' to Germany.................... 112
Got Them Blues 68
The Hesitating Blues 26
Hesitation Blues 54
House of David Blues 70
I Know You, Rider 56
Jay Gould's Daughter 64

Joe Turner......................... 113
Joe Turner Blues..................... 30
The Long-Line Skinner Blues 84
The Memphis Blues 13
Mule Skinner Blues 110
Poor Lazarus........................ 80
A Real Slow Drag 78
St. James Infirmary 104
St. Louis Blues 3
San Francisco Bay Blues 37
Shoeboot's Serenade 21
Silicosis Blues 88
Sportin' Life Blues 90
Stagolee 72
Stealin', Stealin' 48
Take Your Fingers Off It 50
Things About Comin' My Way 92
Unemployment Compensation Blues....... 74
Wanderin'.......................... 106
Weave Room Blues 76
White House Blues.................... 41
Winnsboro Cotton Mill Blues 34
Worried Blues 96
Yellow Dog Blues 17
You Don't Know My Mind 98

St. Louis Blues

"Well, they say that life begins at forty—I wouldn't know—but I was forty the year 'St. Louis Blues' was composed, and ever since then my life has . . . revolved around that composition." (W. C. Handy)

By W. C. Handy
(1914)

I hate to see ___ the eve-nin' sun go down, ___
Feel-in' to mor-row like ___ I feel to-day, ___

Hate to see ___ the eve-nin' sun go down, ___
Feel to-mor-row like ___ I feel to-day, ___

'Cause ___ my ba-by he done left this town. ___
I'll pack my trunk ___ make my get a-

3

Beale Street Blues

'... the wolves that had been yapping at Beale Street ever since I could remember finally caught up with their victim. Backed by excursion boat operators who wanted to draw the liquor trade, and shady characters who hoped to enjoy even bigger profits from illicit business, the reformers eventually prevailed, passing a local option law for Memphis. That was a calamity. Imagine Pee Wee's closing at twelve o'clock at night! Imagine Beale Street without liquor." (W. C. Handy)

Words and Music by
W. C. Handy (1916)

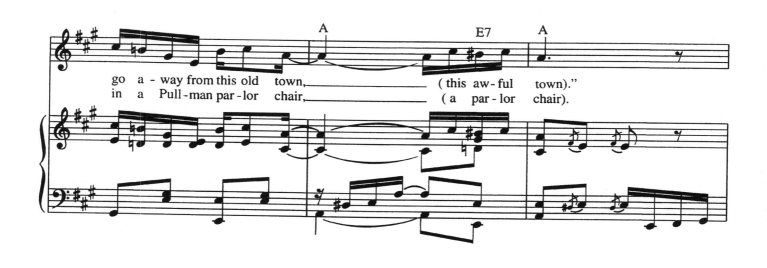

The Memphis Blues

In 1909, W. C. Handy's band was hired to boost the campaign of Edward H. Crump, who was running for mayor of Memphis. Handy dusted off an anti-Crump song, which soon became the hit tune of the election. Crump was elected and eventually got a boulevard leading to the Mississippi River named after him.

By W. C. Handy (1912)

Yellow Dog Blues

"We dusted off the old number that I had written under the title of *Yellow Dog Rag* and republished it as *Yellow Dog Blues* . . . A few weeks later a Texan wrote that he had sold more *Yellow Dog Blues* records than anything in the history of his business which he had conducted from the beginning of the phonograph industry." (W. C. Handy)

The "Yellow Dog" is the Yazoo Delta Railroad.

Words and Music by
W. C. Handy
(1914)

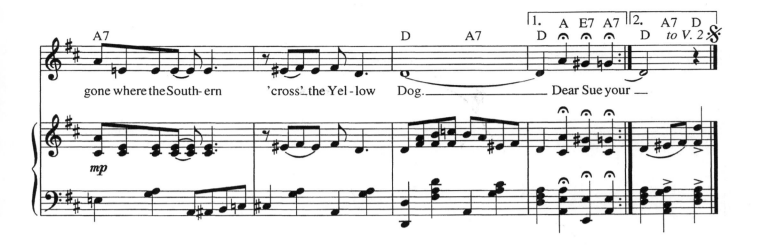

gone where the South-ern 'cross' the Yel-low Dog._____ Dear Sue your

Shoeboot's Serenade

"A white musician expressed doubt of my ability to write or even read music. I coldly, but politely, suggested to him that if he would give me a classical melody, I would promptly give it a Negro setting, both words and music. He said, "See what you can do with *Schubert's Serenade*." (W. C Handy)

Words and Music by
W. C. Handy (1915)

The Hesitating Blues

Blues singers all over the south sang their versions of a "hesitating" blues. A traditional example of this song is *Hesitation Blues*.

Words and Music by
W. C. Handy 1915

Joe Turner Blues

They tell me Joe Turner's come and gone.
They tell my Joe Turner's come and gone.
Got my man and gone.

W. C. Handy took this traditional three-line blues about prison life in Memphis and Nashville and expanded it into a larger and more complex creation. The original song is *Joe Turner*.

Words and Music by
W. C. Handy (1915)

Winnsboro Cotton Mill Blues

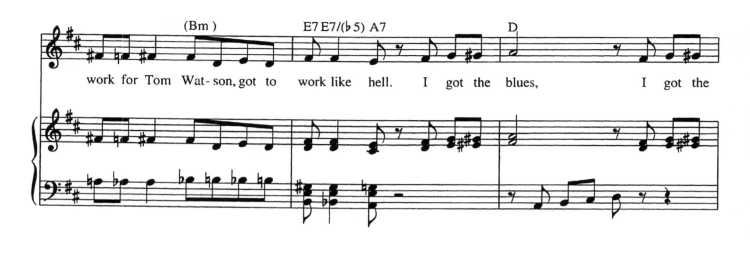
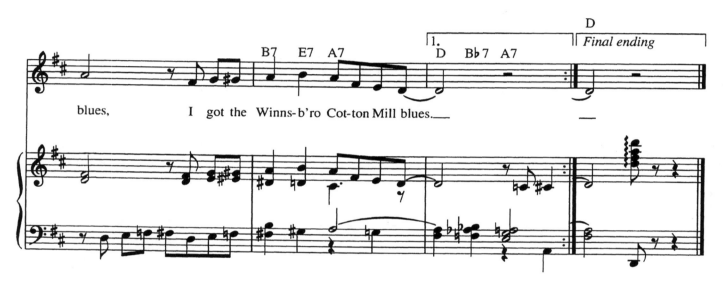

When I die, don't bury me at all,
Just hang me up on the spool room wall.
Place a knotter in my right hand,
So I can keep on spoolin' in the promised land.
Chorus

When I die, don't bury me deep,
Bury me down on 600 Street.
Place a bobbin in each hand,
So I doff in the promised land.
Chorus

White House Blues

President William McKinley was shot on September 6, 1901 in Buffalo, New York, by Leon Zolgotz, an anarchist. Theodore Roosevelt assumed the presidency on September 14, 1901.

Oh it's look here you rascal see what you done,
You shot my husband and I got your gun.
I'm takin' you back to Washington.

Oh the doc come a-running took off his specs,
Said, "Mr. McKinley better cash in your checks,
Your're bound to die, bound to die."

Oh Roosevelt in the White House doin' his best,
McKinley in the graveyard takin' a rest.
He's gone, long gone.

The engine she whistled all down the line,
Blowin' at every station, "McKinley is dyin'."
From Buffalo to Washington.

Roosevelt in the White House, drinkin' out a silver cup,
McKinley in the graveyard, he'll never wake up,
He's gone a long, old time.

Frankie and Johnny went walking, Johnny in his brand new suit.
"Oh, good Lord," said Frankie, "Don't my Johnny man look cute?" *Chorus*

Johnny said, "I've got to leave you, but I won't be very long,
Don't wait up for me, honey, or worry while I'm gone." *Chorus*

Frankie went down to the corner to get a bucket of beer.
She said to the fat bartender, "Has my lovin' man been here?" *Chorus*

"Well, I ain't gonna tell you no story, I ain't gonna tell you no lie,
I saw your Johnny 'bout an hour ago with a gal named Nellie Bly." *Chorus*

Frankie pulled out her six-shooter, pulled out her old forty-four.
Her gun went rooty-toot-toot-toot, and Johnny rolled over the floor *Chorus*

"Oh, roll me over so easy; oh, roll me over so slow,
Oh, roll me over easy, boys, for my wounds, they hurt me so" *Chorus*

Frankie got down on her knees, took Johnny into her lap.
She started to hug and to kiss him, but there was no bringing him back. *Chorus*

"Oh, get me a thousand policemen, and throw me into your cell,
'Cause I've shot my Johnny so dead, I know I'm going to hell." *Chorus*

Roll out your rubber-tired carriage. Roll out your old-time hack.
There's twelve men going to the graveyard and eleven coming back. *Chorus*

The judge said to the jury, "It's plain as plain can be;
This woman shot her lover, it's murder in the second degree." *Chorus*

Now, it was not murder in the second degree, and it was not murder in the third,
The woman simply dropped her man, like a hunter drops a bird. *Chorus*

Frankie mounted to the scaffold as calm as a girl can be,
And turning her eyes to heaven, she said, "Nearer, my God, to Thee." *Chorus*

Now, this story has no moral–this story has no end.
But a man's the cause of all trouble ever since the world began. *Chorus*

Backwater Blues

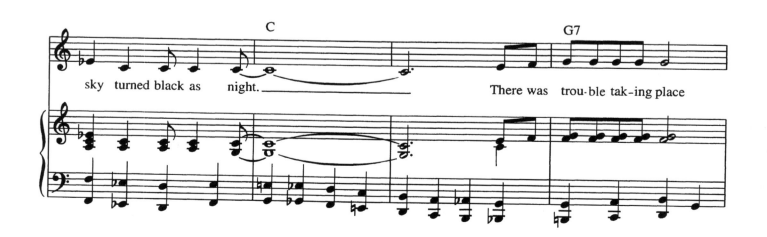

Well, it thundered and it lightened and the winds began to blow, (2)
There was thousands of people didn't have no place to go.

I woke up this morning, couldn't even get out my door, (2)
Enough trouble to make a poor boy wonder where he gonna go.

Alabama Bound

Oh don't you leave me here,
(Oh, don't you leave me here.)
Oh, don't you leave me here,
(Oh, don't you leave me here.)
But if you must go 'way anyhow,
Leave me a dime for beer,
(Leave me a dime for beer.)

Oh, don't you be like me,
(Oh, don't you like me.)
Oh, don't you be like me,
(Oh, don't you be like me.)
Drink your good cherry wine every day,
And let the whisky be,
(And let the whisky be.)

Oh, well your hair don't curl,
(Oh, well your hair don't curl.)
Oh, well your hair don't curl,
(Oh, well your hair don't curl.)
Well, if you don't want me, sweet polly Ann,
Well, I don't want you,
(Well, I don't want you.)

Repeat first verse

Stealin', Stealin'

The woman I'm a-lovin', she's just my height and size,
She's a married woman, come to see me sometime;
If you don't believe I love you,
  Look what a fool I've been.
If you don't believe I'm sinkin',
  Look what a hole I'm in.   *Chorus*

Take Your Fingers Off It

*Verse begins with the opening 8 measures,
and ends with the last 4 measures of verse one.*

Take your fingers off it...
A nickel is a nickel, a dime is a dime,
A house full of children, none of them's mine,
Take your fingers off it...

Empty Bed Blues

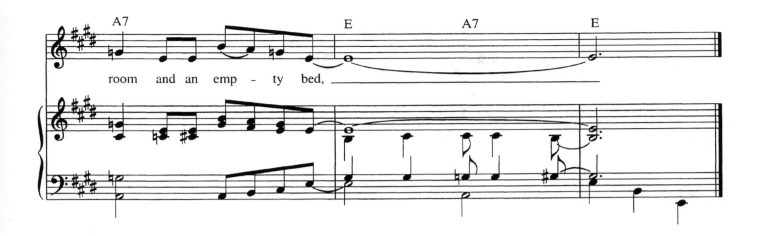

He's a coffee grinder-grinding all the time, (2)
He can grind my coffee, 'cause he's got a brand-new grind.

He came home one evening with his spirit 'way up high, (2)
What he had to give me made me wring my hands and cry.

Well, he knows how to thrill me, and I told my girl friend, Lou, (2)
And the way she's raving she must have gone and tried it too.

If you get good loving, never go and spread the news (2)
Gals will double-cross you and leave you with the Empty Bed Blues.

Hesitation Blues

Well, the eagle on the dollar says, "In God we trust,"
Woman wants a man, she wants to see a dollar first. *Chorus*

Well, you hesitate by ones, and you hesitate by twos.
Angels up in heaven singing hesitation blues. *Chorus*

I Know You, Rider

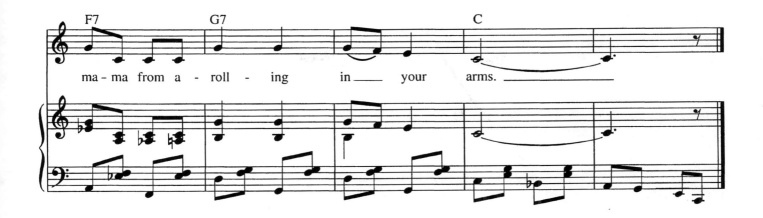

I'm goin' down the road where I can get more decent care, (2)
Goin' back to my used-to-be rider 'cause I don't feel welcome here.

I'm goin' down to the river, set in my rocking chair, (2)
And if the blues don't find me, gonna rock away from here.

I know my baby sure is bound to love me some, (2)
'Cause he throws his arms around me like a circle 'round the sun.

Lovin' you baby, just as easy as rollin' off a log, (2)
But if I can't be your woman, I sure ain't gonna be your dog.

I laid down last night tryin' to take a rest, (2)
But my mind kept rambling like the wild geese in the West.

Sun gonna shine in my back yard some day, (2)
And the wind gonna rise up, baby, blow my blues away.

Brown's Ferry Blues

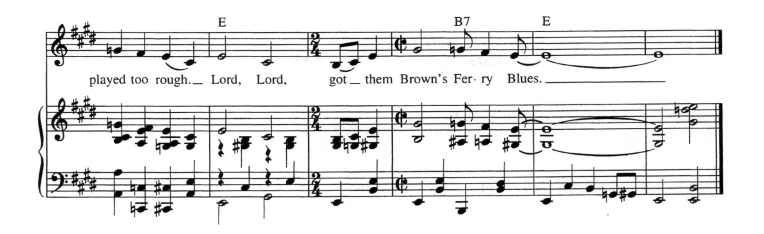

Two old maids a-sitting in the sand,
Each one wishing that the other was a man.
    Lord, Lord, got those Brown's Ferry blues.
Two old maids done lost their style,
If you want to be lucky you got to smile.
    Lord, Lord, got those Brown's Ferry blues.

Early to bed and early to rise,
And your gal goes out with other guys.
    Lord, Lord, got those Brown's Ferry blues.
If you don't believe me, try it yourself,
Well, I tried it and I got left.
    Lord, Lord, got those Brown's Ferry blues.

Hard luck poppa standing in the rain,
If the world was corn he couldn't buy grain.
    Lord, Lord, got those Brown's Ferry blues.
Hard luck poppa standing in the snow,
His knees knock together but he's raring to go.
    Lord, Lord, got those Brown's Ferry blues.

Deep River Blues

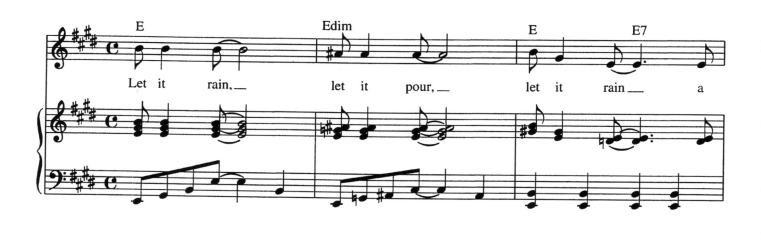

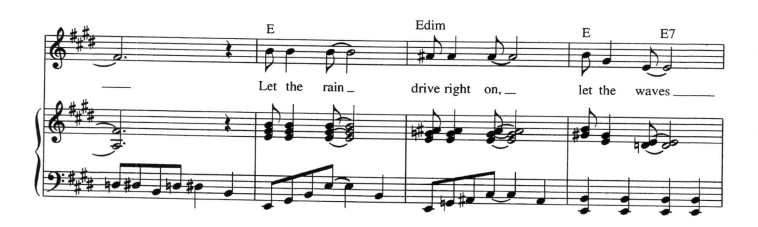

My old gal done me wrong,
That is why I sing this song___
And I've got them deep river blues.
There ain't no one to cry for me,
That's why I'm blue, don't you see?
And I've got them deep river blues.

Give me back my old boat,
I'm gonna sail, if she'll float___
'Cause I've got them deep-river blues.
I'm goin' back to Mussel Shoals,
Times are better there, I'm told___
'Cause I've got them deep-river blues.

If my boat sinks with me,
I'll go down, don't you see___
'Cause I've got them deep-river blues.
Now I'm goin' to say goodbye,
And if I sink just let me die___
'Cause I've got them deep-river blues.

Ain't No More Cane On The Brazis

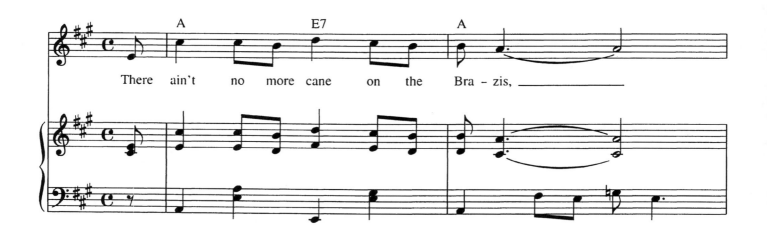
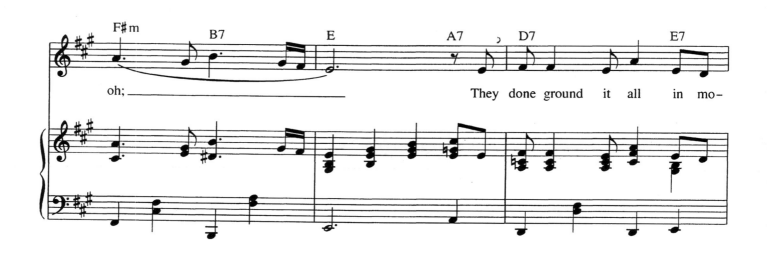
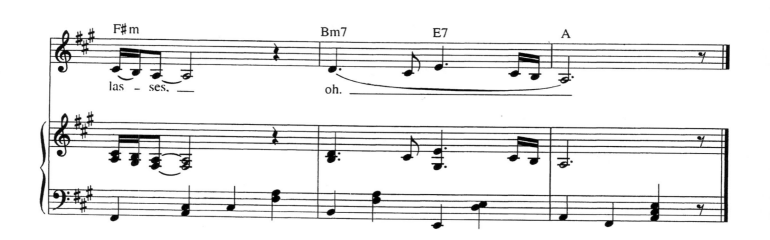

Well, the captain standing and crying...
Well, it's getting so cold, my row's behind...

Cap'n, doncha do me like you did poor Shine...
You drive that bully till he went stone-blin'...

Cap'n, cap'n, you must be blind...
Keep on hollering and I'm almost flying...

Ninety-nine years so jumping long...
To be here rolling and cain't go home...

If had a sentence like ninety-nine years...
All the dogs on the Brazis won't keep me here...

B'lieve I'll do like old Riley...
Ol' Riley walked the big Brazis...

Well, the dog-sergeant got worried and couldn't go...
Ol' Rattler went to howling 'cause the tracks too old...

Oughta come on the river in nineteen four...
You could find a dead man on every turn row...

Oughta come on the river in nineteen ten...
They was driving the women just like the men...

Some in the building and some on the farm.
Some in the graveyard, and some going home...

Wake up, lifetime, hold up your head...
Well, you may get a pardon and you may drop dead...

Go down, Ol' Hannah, doncha rise no more...
If you rise in the morning bring Judgment Day...

Jay Gould's Daughter

Joe Gould (1863-1892) was one of the great railway "robber barons" of the 19th century. He controlled numerous railways, including the Erie and the Union Pacific. By 1880, he was in virtual control of 10,000 miles of railway, about one-ninth of the railway mileage of the United States at that time. His daughter, Helen (1868-1938) became widely known as a philanthropist for her gifts to American army hospitals in the Spanish-American War (1898) and for her many contributions to New York University.

Casey Jones was a good engineer,
He told his fireman not to fear,
All he needed was water and coal;
Put your head out the window, see the drivers roll.
Drivers roll, drivers roll,
Put your head out the window, see the drivers roll.

When we got within a mile of the place,
Old Number One stared us right in the face;
The conductor pulled his watch, and mumbled and said,
"We may make it but we'll all be dead.
All be dead, all be dead,
We may make it but we'll all be dead."

As the two locomotives was about to bump,
The fireman prepared to make his jump;
The engineer blew the whistle, and the fireman bawled,
"Please, Mr. Conductor, won't you save us all?
Save us all, save us all,
Please, Mr. Conductor, won't you save us all?"

O ain't it a pity, ain't it a shame?
The six-wheel driver had to bear the blame.
Some were crippled, and some were lame,
And the six-wheel driver had to bear the blame.
Bear the blame, bear the blame,
And the six-wheel driver had to bear the blame.

Jay Gould's daughter said before she died:
"There's one more road I'd like to ride."
"Tell me, daughter, what can it be?"
It's the Southern Pacific and the Santa Fe.
Santa Fe, Santa Fe
It's the Southern Pacific and the Santa Fe."

Jay Gould's daughter said before she died,
"Father, fix the blind so the bums can't ride;
If ride they must, let them ride the rod,
Let 'em put their trust in the hands of God.
Hands of God hands of God,
Let 'em put their trust in the hands of God."

All Night Long

66

If I live and don't get killed,
I'll make my home in Louisville.
In Louisville, in Louisville,
If I live and don't get killed.

I'd rather be dead and in my grave,
Than in this town, treated this way.
Treated this way, treated this way,
Than in this town, treated this way.

If anyone asks you who wrote this song,
Tell 'em I did – I sing it all night long.
All night long, all night long,
Tell 'em I did – I sing it all night long.

Freight Train Blues

My daddy was a fireman and my mammy dear
Was the only daughter of an engineer.
My sweetie is a brakeman and it ain't no joke
It's a shame the way she keeps a poor man broke. *Chorus*

Know I'm old enough to quit this runnin' around,
Tried a hundred times to settle down.
Every time I find a place I'd like to stay,
Freight train whistle sends me on my way. *Chorus*

House of David Blues

Gee but ain't it grand, don't you hear that band
Play those House of David Blues.
All the folks in town are gath'rin' around,
See the funny things they do.
Domineckeer rooster and a bow-legged hen,
They go together but they ain't no kin.
Gee but ain't it grand, don't you hear that band,
Play those House of David Blues.

Stagolee

Oh, Billy de Lyon shot six bits,
Stagolee bet he'd pass,
Stagolee out with his "forty-four,"
Said, "You done shot your last."
When you lose your money,
Learn to lose.

Well, a woman came a–running,
Fell down on her knees,
Crying, "Oh Mr. Stagolee,
Don't shoot my brother, please."
When you lose your money,
Learn to lose.

It was way down in the gambling hall,
Fighting on the floor,
Old Stagolee pulled the trigger
Of that smoking "forty-four."
When you lose your money,
Learn to lose.

Well, you talking about some gamblers,
You ought to seen Richard Lee,
He bet one thousand dollars,
Then he come out on a three.
Crying, when you lose your money,
Learn to lose.

Oh, Billy de Lyon said to Stagolee,
"Please don't take my life,
I got two little babes
And a darling loving wife."
When you lose your money,
Learn to lose.

Now what do I care about your two little babes,
Your darling loving wife,
Boy, you done took my stetson hat
And I'm bound to take your life.
When you lose your money,
Learn to lose.

Gentlemen of the jury,
What do you think about that,
Old Stagolee killed Billy de Lyon
About a five dollar Stetson hat.
When you lose your money,
Learn to lose.

Well the judge said, "Mr. Stagolee,
Mr. Stagolee,
I'm gonna lock your body up
And set your spirit free."
When you lose your money,
Learn to lose.

Unemployment Compensation Blues

Words & Music by
Les Pine

© 1949 by The Sing Out Corporation (transferred from People's Song, Inc., and Sing Out Inc. 1957) renewed. All Rights Reserved.

I've got those unemployment compensation – "Please fill out an application" – blues.
I've got those "State your weekly minimum, you don't wanna work you bum" – blues.
And when I'm through with my weekly routine, I spend my money on thorazine,
I've got those – by the time I get my check, I become a nervous wreck – blues.

I've got those unemployment compensation, it ain't worth the aggravation blues.
I've got those – "Won't you wait, just have a chair. Nothin' my frigidaire" – blues.
I'm tired of feelin' like a jerk, all I want is a chance to work,
And lose those – out–of–work humiliation, unemployment compensation – blues.

Weave Room Blues

Words and Music by
Dorsey Dixon

© 1966 by The Sing Out Corporation (transferred from Sing Out Inc.) All Rights Reserved.

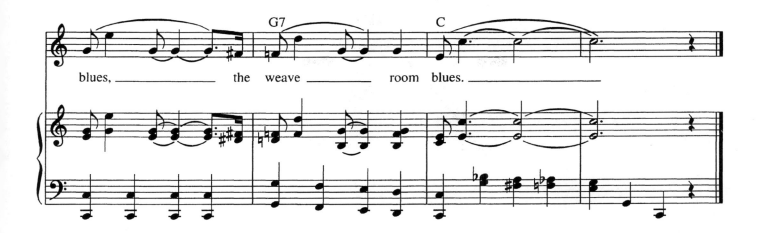

With your looms a-slamming, shuttles bouncing on the floor,
And when you flag your fixer, you can see that he is sore.
I'm trying to make a living but I'm thinking I will lose,
But I'm a-getting nothing but them weave-room blues. *Chorus*

The harness eyes are breaking and the doubles coming through:
The devil's in your alley and he's coming after you;
Our hearts are aching, let us take a little booze,
For we're simply dying with them weave-room blues. *Chorus*

Slam-outs, bread-outs, know-ups by the score,
Cloth all rolled back and piled up in the floor,
The bats are running ends, the strings are hanging to your shoes,
We're simply dying with them weave-room blues. *Chorus*

A Real Slow Drag

"Scott Joplin . . . has created an original type of music in which he employs syncopation in a most artistic and original manner. It is in no sense rag-time, but of that peculiar quality of rhythm which Dvorak used so successfully in the "New World Symphony" . . . It is always a pleasure to meet with something new in music . . ."

From a review of Joplin's opera, *Treemonisha*, which appeared in the June 24, 1911 issue of "The American Musician." *A Real Slow Drag* is the finale of the opera.

Words and Music by
Scott Joplin

Poor Lazarus

Oh, the deputy 'gin to wonder, where in the world could he find him, (2)
Well, I don't know, Lord, Lord, I just don't know, Lord, Lord.

Oh, they found poor Lazarus way out between two mountains, (2)
And they blowed him down, Lord, Lord, and they blowed him down, Lord, Lord.

Old Lazarus told the deputy he had never been arrested, (2)
By no one man, Lord, Lord, by no one man, Lord, Lord.

So they shot poor Lazarus – shot him with a great big number, (2)
Number forty–five, Lord, Lord, number forty–five, Lord, Lord.

Lazarus told the deputy, "Please gimme a cool drink of water." (2)
"Just before I die, Lord, Lord, just before I die, Lord, Lord."

Been In the Pen So Long

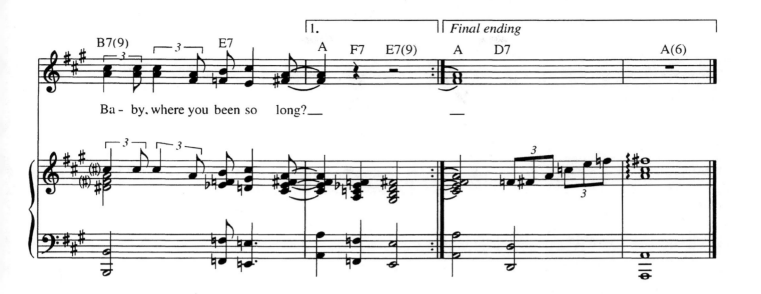

Awful lonesome, all alone and blue,
Awful lonesome, all alone and blue.
All alone and blue,
No one to tell my troubles to,
Baby, where you been so long?
Baby, where you been so long?

Some folks crave for Memphis, Tennessee,
Some folks crave for Memphis, Tennessee,
Some folks crave
For Memphis, Tennessee,
But New Orleans is good enough for me,
New Orleans is good enough for me.

The Long-Line Skinner Blues

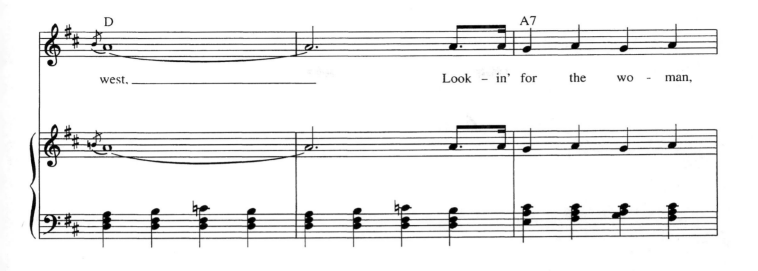

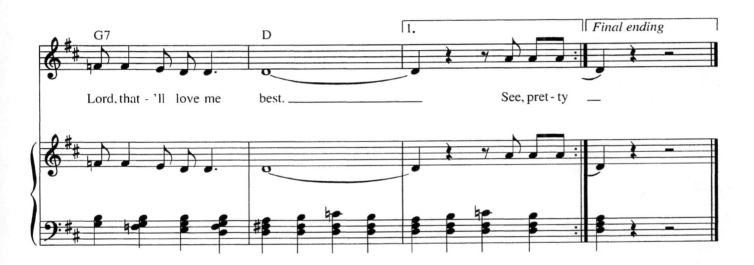

See, pretty mama, pretty mama, look what you done done.
You made your daddy love you now your man done done.
I'm a long-line skinner and home's out west,
Lookin' for the gal, Lord, that'll love me best.

I'm way down in the bottom skinning mules for Johnny Ryan,
Puttin' my initials, honey, on a mule's behind.
With my long whip line, babe. With my long whip-line–
Lookin' for woman who can ease my worried mind.

When the weather it gets chilly, gonna pack up my line,
'Cause I ain't skinnin' mules, Lord, in the wintertime.
Yes, I'm a long-line skinner and my home's out west,
And I'm lookin' for the woman, Lord, that'll love me the best.

Darlin'

Asked my captain for the time of day, darlin', darlin',
Asked my captain for the time of day, darlin', darlin',
Asked my captain for the time of day,
He got so mad he threw his watch away—darlin', darlin'.

Fight my captain and I'll land in jail, darlin', darlin',
Fight my captain and I'll land in jail, darlin', darlin',
Fight my captain and I'll land in jail,
Nobody 'round to go my bail—darlin', darlin'.

If I'd a-had my weight in lime, darlin', darlin',*
If I'd a-had my weight in lime, darlin', darlin',
If I'd a-had my weight in lime,
I'd have whipped that captain till he went stone blind—darlin', darlin'.

If I'd a-listened to what my mama said, darlin', darlin',
If I'd a-listened to what my mama said, darlin', darlin',
If I'd a-listened to what my mama said,
I'd be home and in my mama's bed—darlin', darlin'.

    If I'd a-known my captain was blind, darlin', darlin',
    If I'd a-known my captain was blind, darlin', darlin',
    If I'd a-known my captain was blind,
    I wouldn't have gone to work till half-past nine—darlin', darlin'.

    *If I were a white man—on even terms for a fair fight.

Silicosis Blues

For years the big mining companies bitterly fought the claims of the coal miners who had developed this dreaded respiratory disease while working in the mines. Often an out-of-court payment of a few hundred dollars would "settle" the case of a man who, after spending most of his life "where the rain never falls and sun never shines," could now look forward to spending his few remaining years as an unproductive invalid.

Words – traditional
Music by Jerry Silverman

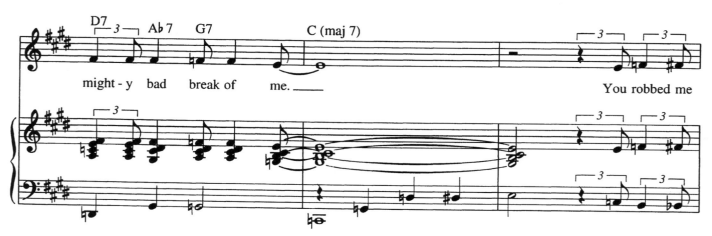

Now, silicosis, you're a dirty robber and a thief.
Silicosis, you're a dirty robber and a thief.
Robbed me of my right to live, and all you brought poor me was grief.

I was there diggin' that tunnel for six bits a day.
I was there diggin' that tunnel for six bits a day.
Didn't know I was diggin' my own grave, silicosis eatin' my lungs away.

I says, "Mama, Mama, Mama, cool my fevered head."
I says, "Mama, Mama, Mama, cool my fevered head."
"I'm gonna leave, my Jesus, God knows I'll soon be dead."

Six bits I got for diggin', diggin' in that tunnel hole.
Six bits I got for diggin', diggin' in that tunnel hole.
Take me 'way from my baby, it sure done wrecked my soul.

Now tell all my buddies, tell all my baby, it sure done see.
Tell all my buddies, tell all my friends you see,
I'm goin' away up yonder, please don't weep for me.

Sportin' Life Blues

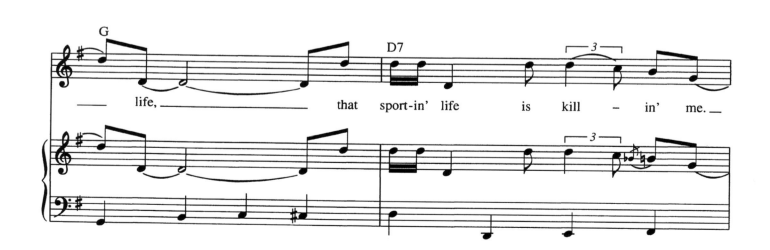

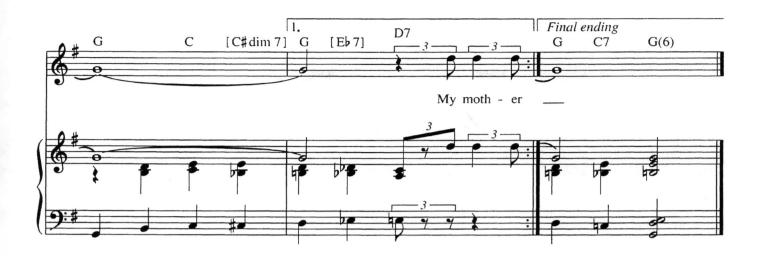

My mother used to say to me,
"So young and foolish, that I can't see."
Ain't got no mother, my sister and brother won't talk to me.

I've been a liar and a cheater too,
Spent all my money on booze and you;
That old night life, that sportin' life is killin' me.

My mother used to say to me,
"So young and foolish, that I can't see.
Ho, Jerry, hey there, Jerry, why don't you change your ways?"

I've been a gambler and a cheater too,
But now it's come my turn to lose,
This old sportin' life has got the best hand, what can I do?

There ain't but one thing that I've done wrong,
Lived this sportin' life, my friend, too long;
I say it's no good, please believe me, please leave it alone.

I'm gettin' tired of runnin' 'round,
Think I will marry and settle down;
That old night life, that sportin' life is killin' me.

Things About Comin' My Way

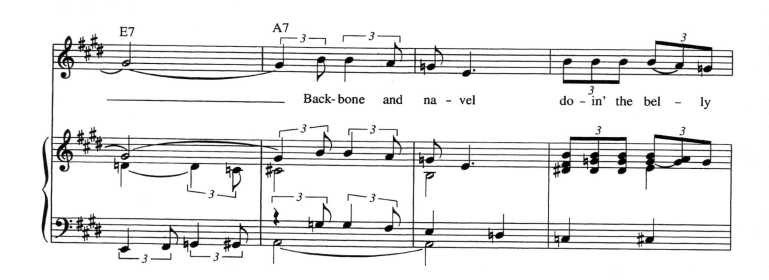

The pot was empty, the cupboard bare,
I said, "Mama, mama, what's goin' on here?" *Chorus*

The rent was due, the light was out,
I said, "Mama, mama, what's it all about?" *Chorus*

Sister was sick, doc wouldn't come,
'Cause we couldn't pay him the proper sum. *Chorus*

Lost all my money, ain't got a dime,
Givin' up this cold world, leavin' it behind. *Chorus*

Work all this summer and all the fall,
Gonna make this Christmas in my overalls. *Chorus*

One of these days–it won't be long,
You'll call my name and I'll be gone.
Final Chorus:
'Cause after all my hard trav'lin',
Things'll be comin' my way.

Got Them Blues

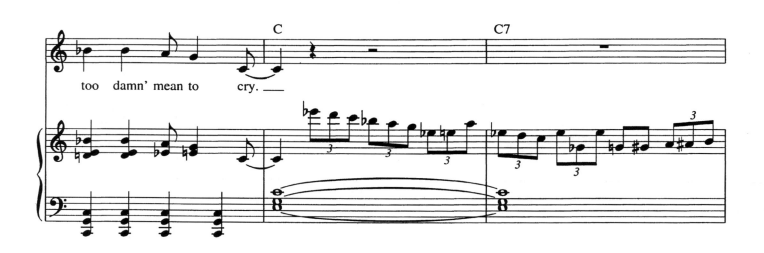

Feel so bad, but I'm too mean, Lordy,
I'm too damn' mean to cry.
Feel so bad, but I'm too damn' mean to cry.
Yes, I feel so awful bad, but I'm too damn' mean to cry
Yes, mean to cry.

Jim Crow hurts, but I'm too mean, Lordy,
I'm too damn' mean to cry.
Jim Crow hurts, but I'm too damn' mean to cry.
Yes, mean old Jim Crow hurts, but I'm too damn' mean to cry
Yes, mean to cry.

Fight like hell, cause I'm too mean, Lordy,
I'm too damn' mean to cry.
Fight like hell 'cause I'm too damn' mean to cry.
Yes, I'm gonna fight like hell, 'cause I'm too damn' mean to cry
Yes, mean to cry.

Worried Blues

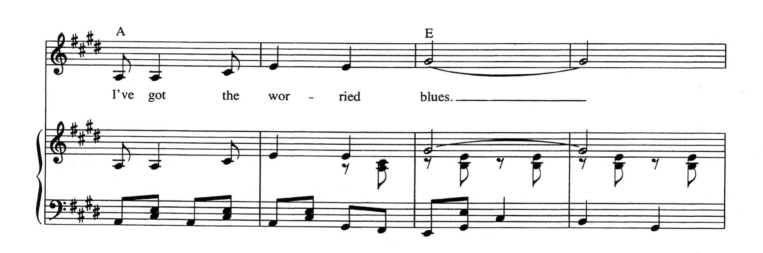

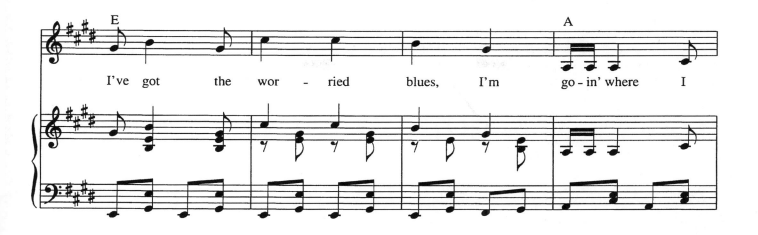

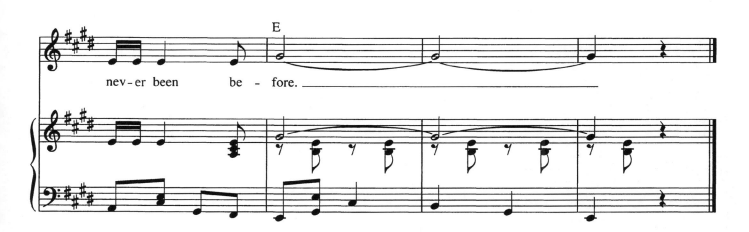

Goin' where I never been beat,
I'm goin' where the chilly winds don't blow,
Goin' where I never been beat, oh, Lord,
Goin' where I never been beat,
I'm goin' where the chilly winds don't blow.

Honey baby, don't leave me now,
Oh, honey baby, don't leave me now,
Honey baby, don't leave me now, oh, Lord,
Honey baby, don't leave me now,
Well, I've got trouble in my mind.

Goin' where the orange blossoms bloom,
I'm goin' where the chilly winds don't blow,
Goin' where the orange blossoms bloom, oh, Lord
Goin' where the orange blossoms bloom,
I'm goin' where I never been before.

I've got the worried blues, Lord,
I've got the worried blues.
I've got the worried blues, oh, Lord,
I've got the worried blues,
I'm goin' where I never been before.

You Don't Know My Mind

A magazine in Buenos Aires, in attempting to define "los blues" for its readers, chose the first verse of this song as a typical example of the genre: *Si, así es querida nena, tú no conoces, mi pensaminto . . . . Cuando crees que estoy riendo, estoy riendo por no llorar.*

You can't tell, you can't tell, you can't tell how I feel.
You can't tell, you can't tell how I feel,
With these cold iron shackles—shackles diggin' in my heel.

You can't see, you can't see, you can't see me now.
You can't see me baby, you can't see me now,
'Cause I'm long-time gone—gone and won't be back nohow.

Easy Rider

An "easy rider" is an unpleasant character who lives well, supported by the efforts of his woman or women.

If I was a catfish, swimmin' in the deep blue sea,
If I was a catfish, swimmin' in the deep blue sea,
I would swim across the ocean, bring my baby back to me.
Well, it's hey, hey, hey, hey, hey.

I'm goin' away, Rider, and I won't be back till fall,
I'm goin' away, Rider, and I won't be back till fall,
And if I find me a good man, I won't be back at all.
Well, it's hey, hey, hey, hey, hey.

Alberta, Let You Hair Hang Low

This beautiful love song ranks with the finest creations in any language and by any composer. It should be sung with slow and tender expressiveness.

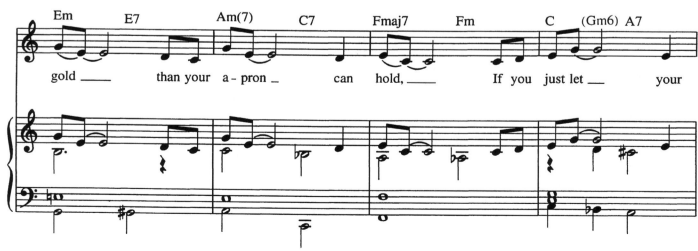

Alberta, what's on your mind?
Alberta, what's on you mind?
You keep me worried, you keep me bothered all the time.
Alberta, what's on your mind?

Alberta, don'cha treat me unkind,
Alberta, don'cha treat me unkind,
Oh, my heart is sad 'cause I want you so bad.
Alberta, don'cha treat me unkind.

St. James Infirmary

On my left stood big Joe McKennedy,
His eyes were bloodshot red.
He turned to the crowd around him,
These were the very words he said.

"I went down to the St. James Infirmary
To see my baby there.
She was stretched out on a long white table,
So pale, so cold and so fair."

Let her go, let her go, God-bless her,
Wherever she may be.
She may search this whole world over,
Never find a man as sweet as me.

When I die, please bury me
In my high-top Stetson hat.
Put a twenty-dollar gold piece on my watch chain,
So the gang'll know I died standing pat.

I want six crap shooters for pall bearers.
Six pretty gals to sing me a song.
Put a jazz band on my hearse wagon
To raise hell as we stroll along.

And now that you've heard my story,
I'll have another shot of booze.
And if anybody happens to ask you,
I've got the St. James Infirmary blues."

East Colorado Blues

This is the hammer that killed John Henry, } 2
But it won't kill me. (3)

Well, John Henry he left his hammer, } 2
Lyin' side the road. (3)

This old hammer fallin' from my shoulder, } 2
The steel goin' down. (3)

When you hear my hammer ringin', } 2
Steel runnin' like lead. (3)

Take this hammer, carry it to the captain, } 2
Yes, tell him I'm gone. (3)

Wanderin'

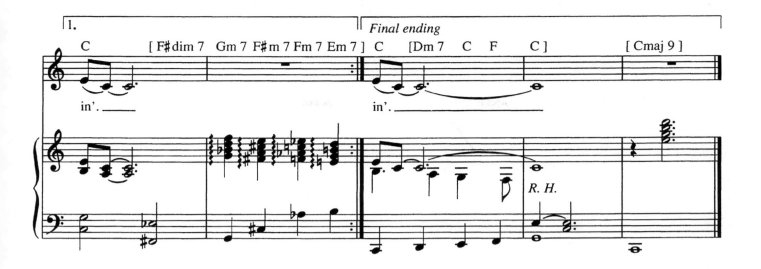

I've been a-wanderin' early and late,
New York city to the Golden Gate.
Chorus

Been a-workin' in the city; been a-workin' on the farm,
And all I've got to show for it is the muscle in my arm.
Chorus

Snakes in the ocean, in the sea,
A redheaded woman made a fool out of me.
Chorus

Boll Weevil Blues

One of the many variants of the same sad story, this song is sometimes referred to as the Ballad of the Boll Weevil.

Farmer take the boll weevil,
Put him in the ice.
Boll weevil say to the farmer,
"You treat me mighty nice."

Farmer take the boll weevil,
He put him in the sand.
Boll weevil say to the farmer,
"You just like a man."

Man said to the old lady,
"What do you think of that?
I got one of them boll weevils
Out of my Stetson hat."

Farmer said to the boll weevil,
"Yes, I wish you well."
He said to the boll weevil,
"I hope you burn in hell."

Boll weevil said to the farmer,
"I'm gonna swing on your gate,
When I get through with your cotton,
You'll sell your Cadillac eight."

Boll weevil said to the farmer,
"I'm gonna treat you mean,
When I get through with your cotton,
You buy no gasoline."

Mule Skinner Blues

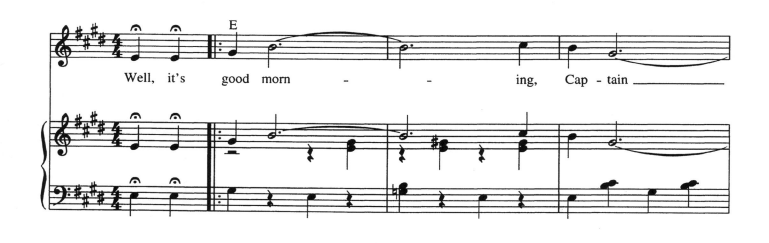
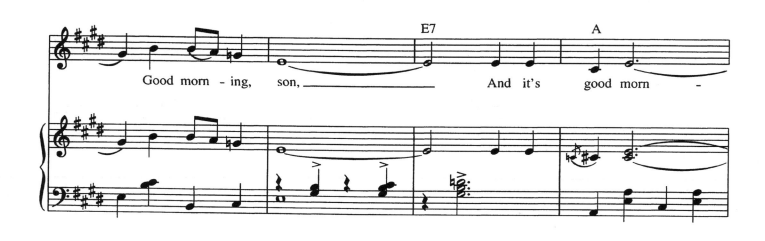

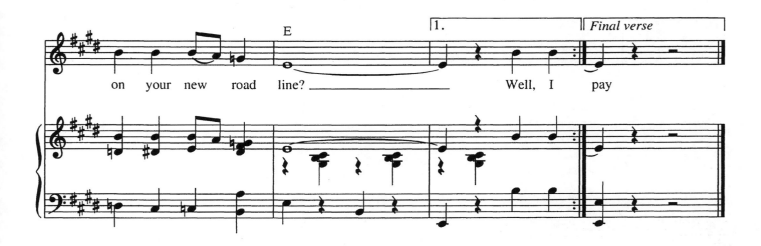

Well, I like to work, I'm rolling all the time;
Yes, I like to work, I'm rolling all the time;
I can carve my initials right on a mule's behind.

Well, it's hey, little water boy, bring your water 'round;
And it's hey, little water boy, bring your water 'round;
If you don't like your job, set that water bucket down.

I'm a-workin' on that new road at a dollar and a dime a day,
Workin' on that new road — dollar and a dime a day;
I got three women waitin' on a Saturday night just a draw my pay.

Goin' to Germany

I'm in the army, there'll be some fighting done,
I'm in the army, there'll be some fighting done,
I'll be back mama when this old war is won.

Please tell me, mama, just what more can I do?
Please tell me, mama, just what more can I do?
'Bout all I know is can't get along with you.

Stay 'way from my window, stop knocking on my door,
Stay 'way from my window, stop knocking on my door,
I got no woman - can't use you anymore.

When you's in trouble I worked and paid your fine,
When you's in trouble I worked and paid your fine,
Now I'm in trouble you don't pay me no mind.

Joe Turner

When Pete Turney became the governor of Tennessee in 1892, he made his brother Joe the "long-chain man." It was Joe Turney's job to transport convicts from Memphis to the Nashville penitentiary. So, when Joe Turney came to town, it was bye-bye for some woman's man. Through a typical folk metamorphosis his name was changed to Joe Turner. This is, perhaps the oldest recorded blues. It is sometime referred to as the "Granddaddy of the Blues."

He come with forty links of chain.
He come with forty links of chain. (Oh, Lordy)
Got my man and gone.

They tell me Joe Turner's come and gone.
They tell me Joe Turner's come and gone. (Oh, Lordy)
Done left me here to sing this song.

Come like he never come before.
Come like he never come before. (Oh, Lordy)
Got my man and gone.

Fare Thee Well

I've got a man and he's long and tall,
Moves his body like a cannon ball.
    Fare thee well, O honey, fare thee well.

'Member one night, a-drizzlin' rain,
Round my heart I felt a pain.
    Fare thee well, O honey, fare thee well.

When I wore my apron low,
Couldn't keep you from my do'.
    Fare thee well, O honey, fare thee well.

Now I wear my apron high,
Scarcely ever see you passing by.
    Fare thee well, O honey, fare thee well.

Now my apron's up to my chin,
You pass my door and you won't come in
    Fare thee well, O honey, fare thee well.

If had listened to what my mama said,
I'd be at home in my mama's bed.
    Fare thee well, O honey, fare thee well.

One of these days, and it won't be long,
Call my name and I'll be gone.
    Fare thee well, O honey, fare thee well.

Careless Love

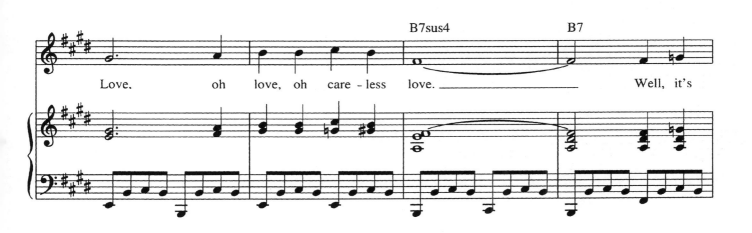

115

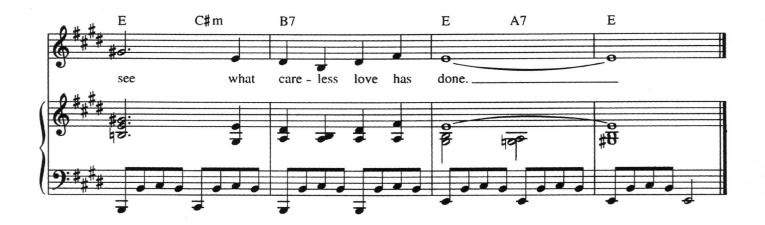

I cried last night and the night before, (3)
Gonna cry tonight and cry no more.

I love my momma and my poppa too, (3)
But I'd leave them both to go with you.

When I wore an apron low, (3)
You'd follow me through rain and snow.

Now I wear my apron high, (3)
You see my door and pass on by.

How I wish that train would come, (3)
And take me back where I come from.

Made in the USA
San Bernardino, CA
05 April 2017